MILLIE VISITS THE LAKE

Created by Lisa Levesque McGloin

Illustrated by Jessica McClure

Acknowledgements

To Allen, Laura and Rebecca for allowing me the privilege to write
this inspirational story about such a beautiful person #stayred

To Millie may you rest in peace surrounded
by all of your flowers and magnificent butterflies.

To Tony, Jamie & Megan for not always thinking your mom is crazy
for wanting to write fun or inspirational stories.

MILLIE

Join Millie on her adventures to visit special friends and places.
Watch as her magical wings change colors depending on her mood,
and sometimes her food, as she shares her stories.
Come along for a visit!

"Good Morning Barkley!" exclaims Millie as she stretches her wings.
"Someone is full of energy this morning," replies Barkley as he stretches
his long limbs and ruffles his leaves. "And where are you off to today?"

"I'm so excited because today is my adventure to the lake and visit with my friend Joy." smiles Millie. "I'm sure you'll have a wonderful time. I can't wait to hear allllllll about it." Barkley says as he waves goodbye.

Millie chooses a purple flower knowing that its Joy's favorite color.
As she drinks her wings slowly change. "Good Morning Wallter,"
she says as she looks over at the stone wall.

"What's so good about it?" Grumbles Wallter "Oh Wallter, don't be so grumpy!"
Millie laughs as she flies off onto her adventure.

As Millie flutters toward the dock, her friend Joy comes running to greet her.
"Hiiiiiii Millieeeeee!" Joy shouts excitedly.

"I'm so glad you came to visit! My mom said the weather is going to be perfect today.
I can show you some of the things my family and I love to do at the lake"
Joy says as Millie lands on her finger.

"I have someone very special for you to meet!" Joy tells Millie. "Zoeyyyyy!"

Out of nowhere, an adorable puppy comes running towards them.
"Come on Zoey, let's show Millie some of the fun things we do!"

"Zoey is learning to swim so she follows my voice. Watch!" And off they go into the water. Joy swims as Zoey follows close behind doing the doggie paddle.

"Good girl Zoey, good girl," Joy repeats as she swims from the dock to the shore and back.

After swimming, Zoey disappears into the flower bed. Suddenly she pops out with a bright new tennis ball. Joy laughs, "I guess it's time to play fetch."

"I teach her fetch by letting her sniff the ball and then place it a few feet away.
Go get the ball Zoey." Zoey runs and fetches the ball to bring back to Joy.
"I place the ball farther and farther away each time."

"She's quite a special puppy, Millie," explains Joy. "Zoey was born blind, so all of the games we play teach her how to use her other senses like hearing and smelling."

"That's amazing Joy, I would have never known! What an incredible family you have to adopt such a special puppy," says Millie.

Joy, Zoey, and Millie head up to the house. "Mom! Dad!
Can we take Zoey and Millie for a boat ride?" shouts Joy.

Zoey turns and runs down the dock to the boat and barks.
"How can we say no to that?" laughs Joy's mom.

Zoey hops up to the front of the boat with her nose in the air sniffing excitedly.

Millie flies alongside the boat as they all enjoy the beautiful sunny day.

When they return from the ride, Joy's mom and dad start cooking dinner on the grill.
Zoey smells the food and sits eagerly next to Joy's dad as he cooks,
hoping for something to drop.

After dinner, they all gather around the fire pit.
Zoey curls up and falls fast asleep near the fire's warmth.

Millie sighs, "I think I better head home before the sun sets. Thanks you so much for sharing your day with me. Now I understand why you love the lake so much, I had a great time!" "Please come visit again soon," says Joy, as her and her family wave goodbye.

As Millie nestles into the crook of Barkley's branch, she yawns and says, "Visiting Joy and her family today was amazing. We had so much fun and there were so many beautiful flowers to play on!" Barkley watches as Millie's eyes grow heavy. "I'm glad you enjoyed your day. Now get some sleep before tomorrow's adventure!"

Even with a disability you can still have JOY in your life!

My very first book of "Millie Adventures" is a dedication to
a special young lady whose physical time with us ended much too soon,
but her impact on many of our lives will never be forgotten.
Upon her departure she left gifts of herself to Donate Life.
One of these was her gift of sight, something that many of us take for granted.
This story is in memory of Melissa, her gift, and her love for her family,
the lake, and of course, Zoey.

Melissa Joy Molin 9/25/1994 – 4/4/2016 will forever be in our hearts.
Keep smiling. #StayRed #youaremisseddearly

The Adventures of Millie is not only a story, character or creation about learning or kindness.
It's my opportunity to spread awareness about the importance of Organ Donation.
Donate Life has had a personal impact on the life of not only my family, but myself.

I was given the Gift of Life by a dear friend,
and that gift has allowed me to continue
my story and be able to share Millie.

A percentage of proceeds from each book sold will be donated to
local Pediatric Transplant hospitals in hopes to make a child's transplant journey a little easier.

Becoming an organ/tissue donor is quite simple.
You many either register at your local DMV upon licensing or renewal,
or you may go to ANY of the following sites.

iPhone users can register by going to their Health app, pressing on the Medical ID, scrolling down
to "Donate Life," and entering their information. Makes sure to press "Done" to see your changes.

https://registerme.org - Fill in your information – click SUBMIT

It's that simple.

http://www.ctorganandtissuedonation.org – select "Register Me" fill in your information - SUBMIT
https://www.donatelife.net – select "Register to be a Donor", fill in your information - SUBMIT

There are over 100,000 people currently on "Wait Lists".
One life can save up to eight (8) lives.

The last page in someone's life may be the beginning or middle of someone else's book.
Please take a moment today and sign up because,

"Tomorrow is not guaranteed, each day is a gift."